A Redneck Christmas Carol

SCROOGE

Published by Crane Hill Publishers
Distributed by Council Oak Books
Printed in China

Library of Congress Cataloging-in-Publication Data available.

ISBN 1-57587-215-3

A Redneck Christmas Carol

SCROOGE

Wrote Up by E.J. Sullivan
Drawed by Ernie Eldredge

CRANE HILL
PUBLISHERS

Jim Bob Marley was sure enough dead and gone. And it was a darn shame, too. Since Jim Bob passed, things just wadn't the same around Ebenezer Scrooge's New and Used Car Lot. 'Bout the only thing that hadn't changed was the sign outside that said, "If You Need Wheels, We Got Deals."

Bubba Cratchit, the only employee old Scrooge had left, couldn't help thinkin' all this, like he did every Christmas Eve. Shoot, Jim Bob Marley wadn't no saint, but when he was alive, they at least used to close the lot early on Christmas Eve and play a little foosball. Sometimes, Jim Bob even opened up the soft drink machine and everybody got them a free Dr. Pepper. Them days was gone for sure.

Nowadays, Scrooge made Bubba work most every holiday and he didn't give nothin' away cheap, let alone free. Here it was after nine o'clock on Christmas Eve and Scrooge was still gripin' about what all they sold that day and not sayin' a word about lettin' Bubba go home.

"Mr. Scrooge, I sure would like to get on home to Earlene and the kids," Bubba said. "I still got to stop on the way and buy a Christmas present for my youngest, Tee-Niney Tim."

"Don't be a dang fool, Cratchit, we still got time to sell two or three more cars," Scrooge practically bit Bubba's head off.

Bubba sat there miserable, thinking about his family, sure nobody else would come in tonight, on Christmas Eve. Shoot, he already sold a used car and two trucks that day anyway. That oughta be enough.

But it wadn't enough for mean old Ebenezer Scrooge. Nothin' was ever enough for Scrooge.

At ten o'clock though, when Bubba asked again to go home, Scrooge give in. "Lazy good for nothin'," he said. "I s'pose you want tomorrow off, too."

"Well it is Christmas," Bubba said.

"Bah dang humbug. Christmas. I ain't payin' you for it. And you better get in here bright and early next day. Now here, Cratchit, here's your wages. Twenty-eight dollars and thirty-three cents. I deducted a dollar for that phone call to your wife and two dollars fer your bathroom privileges. Don't spend it all in one place."

Bubba took the money and left Scrooge's New and Used. It was rainin' hard. Good thing, or somebody mighta noticed that tear in his eye. What could he do with twenty-eight dollars and thirty-three cents? It was too late now to buy anythin' nice for poor little Tee-Niney Tim, even if he could afford to.

Bubba started up his pickup and chugged on home to Paradise Acres. On the way he stopped at the 7-Eleven and bought Moon Pies, Slim Jims, and Nehi's for the kids. For somethin' special for Sister, he bought a lucky rabbit's foot dyed pink, her favorite color. For Junior, he bought a Dale Earnhardt tee-shirt. Tater got a Crimson Tide shot glass — Bubba figured he could keep pennies in it. And for the youngest Cratchit, little Tee-Niney Tim, Bubba bought a giant-size pack of plastic worms, the kind with the smell fish cain't resist. For Earlene, he spent a whole three dollars on a silk rose they had for sale by the cash register.

Meanwhile, Ebenezer Scrooge put on his raincoat. He didn't want to get his new lime green polyester three-piece suit wet, or get mud on them nice new white shoes that was on sale down to Buford's New Deal Department Store. If there was anybody around to see, he mighta looked silly tippy-toeing around the puddles in the lot of Scrooge's New and Used over to his brand new Cadillac. Lucky for Scrooge, there wadn't nobody around.

His car started with a purr. Grumblin' all the way, Scrooge drove himself on home to his big old plantation-style brick house with the big white pillars on the front, and two stone lions guardin' the drive. He lived there all alone, and that was just the way he liked it. Havin' other people around all the time just messed up your stuff.

As he was pullin' into the garage Scrooge thought for just a minute he saw the face of his deceased partner, Jim Bob Marley, where the hood ornament of the Cadillac shoulda been. Marley seemed like he was callin' out to him, shoutin' like or hollerin' a warning. But when Scrooge shook his head and rubbed his eyes, he had to tell himself he was just so tired he was seein' things.

Scrooge fed himself a fine steak dinner, got into his long johns, and crawled into his big four-poster bed. The next thing he knew he was sound asleep. But it seemed like he was havin' some strange kinda dream. There was someone standin' at the foot of his bed.

"What the!..." he yelled.

The figure at the end of the bed was...well it was see-through. It sure looked a heck of a lot like a ghost. And yet it had a mighty powerful presence. It was a man, dazzlin' in his white jewel-studded jumpsuit, slicked-back black pompadour hairstyle, and long sideburns. An electric guitar hung from a strap around his neck. He swung his hips wild-like and mumbled somethin' into a portable microphone about burnin' love....Was it? Could it be? Could it really be?

"Th-th-the K-k-king?" Scrooge stammered, thunderstruck.

"Naw man, I'm just a bad impersonator," the spirit said.

"You ain't Elvis?"

"I told ya, I ain't even a good lookalike."

"Ya look just like him to me...." Scrooge argued, forgettin' for a minute he was talkin' to a ghost.

"Put your glasses on man," the ghost said. "And plug in your hearin' aid. I cain't even sing worth a dang. That's why I'm still here hauntin' folks like you. To pay for all them really bad performances I gave whilst I was a real man here on earth."

Scrooge put on his glasses and hearing aid. Sure enough, this was one really bad Elvis impersonator. "You stink!" Scrooge exclaimed.

"Never mind that. I'm the Ghost of Christmas Past, and I'm here to show you things. Come with me, old buddy." The ghost took him by the hand and suddenly Scrooge was back in time, in the little town of Pot Likker, Mississippi, where he grew up.

"Why, there's my maw and paw and… th-there's Tammy Sue Bledsoe! At the church Christmas party!" Sure enough, there was the sweetheart of Scrooge's past, shyly agreeing to dance with a much younger Ebenezer Scrooge.

As Scrooge and the ghost watched, Tammy Sue and young Ebenezer danced in the candlelighted church fellowship hall. The town's best fiddler played his best waltz for them. They gazed into each other's faces. Then the music ended. After a quiet conversation, Tammy Sue left the church with tears in her eyes.

"You done broke that girl's heart, Ebenezer Scrooge," said the bad Elvis impersonator.

"I wanted to make my fortune," whined Scrooge.

"Yeah, you put material gain over true love," said the ghost.

Scrooge could only look on the scene in silence, his own heart breakin' all over again.

Next thing he knew he was back in his bed at home, alone.

"Whew, musta been that steak dinner," Scrooge muttered as he tossed and turned over in bed. "Shoulda taken me a powder 'fore I went to sleep."

But he didn't have no kinda chance to get back to sleep. There was now somebody else standin' at the end of his bed. She looked a heck of a lot like a waitress, or maybe a beauty operator. Or wait a minute. Didn't this lady have a song on the country and western radio? Scrooge only knew one thing. She sure had big hair.

And the more he looked, the taller she got. She grew and grew and her hair got bigger and bigger until it touched the stars. Her dress changed from a pretty pastel cotton uniform to a shimmery white cloud to a beautiful blue and white spangled gown that, well, Scrooge had to admit, she rather attractively filled.

"Hi honey," she said. "I'm the Ghost of Christmas Present."

Before Scrooge could say a word the ghost had whisked him off to the Paradise Acres mobile home park. Scrooge found himself side by side with the Ghost of Christmas Present, peeking in the window of the Cratchit home.

There he saw, hunkered around the space heater, the Cratchit family: Bubba, Earlene, their children Junior, Sister, and Tater, their faithful dog Blue...and last but not least, riding on Bubba's shoulder carrying a tiny crutch, the baby of the family, Tee-Niney Tim.

"What's wrong with the child?" Scrooge whispered to the ghost, seeing the tiny boy's leg in a homemade cast.

"Busted his leg trying to rescue Old Mrs. Anderson's cat from a tree," whispered the ghost. "Bless his tee-niney heart. Bubba and Earlene had to set his leg theirselves, seeing as how you don't give 'em any insurance and you don't pay Bubba hardly enough to breathe."

"Oh," said Scrooge.

But the little boy's problems didn't seem to put no damper on the Cratchits' Christmas spirits. Earlene was servin' up a big platter of franks and beans. She'd put some pretty sprigs of holly all around the edge of the platter, and there was Moon Pies and Nehi's for dessert.

All the little Cratchits cheered when they saw their mama bring out the platter, and they made ready to sit down to the table in front of the space heater to eat. Behind them, they'd put up a tree Bubba chopped down in the woods, and they decorated it with whatever all they could find around the house: Some old fishin' lures, beads from one of Sis's necklaces, some spray-painted pop tops little Tater made all by hisself. Heck, ole Blue even contributed one of his bones.

"Wait, everyone," little Tee-Niney Tim chirped up from his place on his daddy's big shoulder. "Let's all give thanks for this Christmas dinner before we sit down to eat."

"You're right, Tim, we should be thankful," said Bubba proudly. "We should thank Mr. Ebenezer Scrooge for this feast."

"Oh please, Bubba. We got nothin' to thank that mean old man for," Earlene sounded cross all of a sudden. "He don't care about us. Why he's tighter than a billy goat's butt in a sandstorm."

"Ma!" all the kids said.

"It's Christmas," piped up Tee-Niney Tim again. "Let's get in the spirit and be thankful, Mama, everybody. God bless us every one!"

It was hard to resist Tee-Niney Tim's bright little face. "God bless us every one!" the Cratchits all chimed in as they dug into their Christmas dinner.

Scrooge moaned. "Ohhh, me. Oh, me. I done been a bad, bad man...."

His own words echoed over and over in his ears as he drifted back through darkness and howlin' wind to his bedroom, where now he truly knew no rest. Scrooge had been wakened to the nature of his sins, and he lay tremblin' and frightened in his bed as it rocked and thrashed like a boat in a storm and the wind whirled 'round him in a tempest.

Above it all he heard a deep, terrifyin' voice. It was the voice of doom, boomin' out his name with authority.

"SCROOGE!"

Scrooge hid under the sheets.

"MR. EBENEZER SCROOGE! YOUR FATE IS CALLING YOU!"

Scrooge had no choice but to peer up through the gloom as the wind whipped the covers off his bed. What he saw chilled him to the bone.

It was a third spirit, dark as night, skeletal and forebodin', with a long poorly shaven evil face and wearin' a droopin' black suit, carryin' a big old black briefcase.

"Are you, aa-re y-yoou the Tax Man?" Scrooge cried out in fear.

The ghost boomed back and the earth shook. "SOME CALL ME DEATH, SOME CALL ME TAXES. SOME CALL ME THE REVENUER MAN. MOST JUST CALL ME THE GHOST OF CHRISTMAS FUTURE!"

There was a flash of lightnin' and a loud clap of thunder. Suddenly Scrooge and the frightful ghost in the big black suit were hunkered in freezin' rain outside the trailer of Bubba Cratchit and his family. But things were now different. The little home was dark and fallin' down. It was quiet inside. There was no Christmas tree, no Christmas cheer. Only Bubba and Earlene, huddled by the space heater. Bubba had his arm around Earlene as she sobbed her heart out.

"What's wrong, Ghost?" Scrooge asked the apparition. "Where's the little child?"

The ghost turned his shadowy features, dark as death, on Scrooge.

"He's gone, Ebenezer Scrooge. And so are you."

With another lightnin' flash and blast of thunder, Scrooge was transported to a lonely graveyard. Crumblin' and untended, the few gravestones had fell into the weeds. As lightnin' brightened the scene for one brief moment, he saw the claw of the ghost pointin' at a big stone that had carved on it, "Here Lies Ebenezer Scrooge. P.S. Who Cares?"

"Ohhh me," Scrooge fell down on the ground in tears. "Please Ghost, make it not true," he begged in a real pitiful voice. "Make it not true. Does it have to happen this way?" He sobbed and the earth soaked wet with his remorse. Scrooge truly wished with all his soul that he had been a different man in life, while he still had a chance.

In the image: HERE LIES EBENEZER SCROOGE P.S. WHO CARES?

After a
while he realized
he could no longer hear
the wind and the rain. The darkness
had commenced to lift. The fearful Ghost of Christmas Future was
gone. In fact, Scrooge was back in his bed, safely under the covers. It
was mornin'.

He looked right quick at his fancy watch on the bedside table — the one that give both the time and the date. It wasn't too late! It was just now Christmas mornin'!

Scrooge pulled on his clothes and fairly flew to his Cadillac. He couldn't get to the Winn-Dixie fast enough. He bought the biggest turkey he could find. He bought the biggest ham he could find. He bought oysters and sausages and eggs and bacon. He bought sweet potatoes and turnip greens and fresh rolls and cornmeal and sweet milk. He bought pineapples and oranges and grapes and walnuts. He bought pecan pies and pumpkin pies and red velvet cake and cobbler. He bought ice cream. He bought candy. He bought Coca-Colas by the case and Nehi's and chewing tobacco and bubble gum. He bought socks and ribbons and razors and lipsticks, flashlights and batteries and antifreeze and 10W-40. He bought everythin' he could think of that a man, woman, or child could want.

He piled it all into his Cadillac and drove as fast as he could out to Paradise Acres. The Cratchits were home! Tee-Niney Tim was there! Bubba Cratchit sure was surprised to answer the door and see mean old Ebenezer Scrooge standin' there, looking a plum fool with his arms full of Winn-Dixie grocery bags and a big cock-eyed grin bustin' all his wrinkles in half.

But Bubba Cratchit sure didn't complain, 'specially when Scrooge presented him with that brand spankin' new Cadillac, "So you can drive Tee-Niney Tim to the doctor in style," Scrooge exclaimed.

But Tee-Niney Tim summed it up for everyone
when he piped up in his little angel-chime voice,

"God bless us, all y'all, every one!"